How to Support Your Pastor

David R. Mains

David C. Cook Publishing Co.

ELGIN, ILLINOIS—WESTON, ONTARIO

HOW TO SUPPORT YOUR PASTOR
© 1980 David R. Mains

All Scripture quotations are from the Revised Standard Version unless otherwise noted.

Published by David C. Cook Publishing Co., Elgin, IL 60120
Cover design by Joe Ragont
Printed in the United States of America
ISBN 0-89191-257-6
LC 80-51275

CONTENTS

The Chapel Talks Series by David Mains

Making Church More Enjoyable
How to Support Your Pastor
How to Resist Temptation
God, Help Us with the Kids
What's Wrong with Lukewarm?
Praying More Effectively
Getting to Know the Holy Spirit
When God Gets Angry with a Nation
A Closer Walk with God
Psalms That Touch Us Where We Live
Making Scripture Yours
I Needed That Encouragement

INTRODUCTION

Most people listen to the radio while they're doing something else. As a broadcaster I'm aware that a person hearing me is probably shaving, fixing breakfast, driving to work, or some similar activity. Being able to keep his or her attention in such a setting is a lot different than preaching to a captive audience.

Therefore, I was dubious as to whether the slow pace of radio with its need for frequent repetition and underscoring each key truth would transfer all that well into print.

To complicate matters further, every time a program is made I must assume many listeners didn't hear what was said the day before. But just the opposite is true when compiling the chapters of a book. They build on one another.

Well, the first series of Chapel talks is now completed. Through the help of others, my broadcast scripts have been made more readable than I thought possible. The greatest thanks for this project goes to my wife, Karen, who put aside her own writing to help me out. Two Chapel of the Air staff members, Ruby Christian and Sharon Morse, also did yeoman duty typing long hours after work and on weekends.

1

WHAT OUR CHURCH REALLY NEEDS

"God, have I lost my vision for a great spiritual awakening among your people?" The fact that I asked myself the question as I was driving home from a meeting surprised me. I had identified with such a burden for so long it never seemed possible I could change. Yet my heart seemed so indifferent of late. Not only had doubts grown regarding whether or not I would ever witness a sweeping moving of God's Spirit among His people, but my fervor seemed to be waning.

"Show me, Father, if I've grown cold," I prayed. "Maybe you want my ministry to have a focus on something other than challenging your people to more than mediocre spiritual achievements. Possibly things aren't as bad throughout your ranks as I've diagnosed and the appropriate word for the day is not 'Return, my people, to your first love.' I certainly don't want to speak thoughts contrary to yours. These last weeks my preaching seems so flat, Father, I can't stand to hear myself."

The ambivalence had actually bothered me for several days before I began to put it into words. More miles were passed in quiet and then I turned on the radio. An unknown minister was preaching, not very well, on the topic of revival. As I listened, in spite of his poor choice of words and his lack of finesse, I soon found my heart deeply moved and tears trickled down my cheeks.

This man was saying what I had stated so many times and the Spirit was now witnessing the truth of it to my inner man. Yes, God is calling his people to greater holiness. There is a much higher standard to meet than that which most believers presently attain. The church has become more like the world than is safe. Extremely affected, I was now crying freely. "Thank you, God," I sobbed, "for again revealing to me how strongly I feel in this matter!"

Two days later the experience was repeated, only this time I was at home listening to a new record by a friend, Ken Medema, a blind singer/composer. "I see America Through the Eyes of Love" was the selection, and once again the Spirit moved on my emotions to verify that he had made this calling an integral part of me.

Yet how to communicate this message which seems so close to God's heart? "That's the frustration I've felt, Father. Either what I'm preaching hasn't been timely or it's too hard for people to grasp. For some reason my message isn't stirring my listeners. Can you give me a better handle for them to hold on to?"

A partial answer to that prayer came. Let me share with you what happened.

Having left a Chicago pastorate to become a part of the Chapel of the Air, my wife and I were in the final process of joining a church in Wheaton, Illinois. There was an emphasis we liked on worship and evangelism and overseas missions. "Do we sense the Lord's presence week after week?" we asked each other before making our final decision. The answer was yes.

We continued our evaluation. "Has the church reached its potential?" Not yet, but its future appears exciting. "Are there any flaws that might restrict these visions from being accomplished?" We agreed that if there were a key lack, it was probably in the area of prayer support. With a congregation dominated by young adults, a tendency to ride on hard work and enthusiasm often predominates. But that's really no match against the forces of the enemy.

"Then maybe a gift we can bring to the body is one of intercessory prayer," I said.

"Especially for the pastors," my wife added.

And all of a sudden, lights began blinking: *"Prayer for the pastors,"* we said, "How critical this will be!"

From firsthand experience, I know such men are targets of the enemy whenever churches manifest signs of real life. Studies of growth patterns reveal that a strong minister is always a key in growing congregations. But do members realize the forces of evil unleashed against such leaders for this very reason? I suspect not!

After almost twelve years of pastoral work in the inner city, I couldn't help but be aware that without a proper prayer covering this church would be in trouble. The devil fights dirty when threatened. In fact, no congregation can accomplish truly vital spiritual ministry without a protective canopy of prayer over its leaders.

That's an area I need to emphasize for a while in my preaching, I thought. Not just prayer in general, but prayer targeted for our ministers. What if I could rally thousands of believers to pray for the particular ministers who touch their lives? And I don't mean just "God-bless-Reverend-Smith-Amen" prayers, but real intercession before God on behalf of such men. That would be a significant breakthrough indeed!

"Forget it. In our situation the minister is almost beyond help," you explain.

I respond, "That's all the more reason to pray!"

Imagine what would happen if on Sunday mornings as people gathered for worship there would be the ordinary sound of believers greeting one another in the foyer. But as you entered the sanctuary the low murmer of people praying by twos and threes throughout the auditorium would be the norm. What if most of the people arrived ten or fifteen minutes earlier so as to insure an unrushed time of talking to God? What would happen if, on the way to church in the car, families prayed together for pastors and teachers and musicians? Or what if some of us trained ourselves to get up early on Sunday morning, not to read the paper but to remind the Lord of his servant's needs? Or what if two or three or more Christians fasted on Saturday so that the presence of the Lord would be felt in power on Sunday? Would there be a difference? The powerful effect of this on the congregation is hardly conceivable.

I'm pinpointing one of the strategic needs in today's religious circles. If we could turn things around in this area who can estimate the immense benefits? I can name minister after minister who's laboring under a heavy burden. Though sometimes humans are responsible, more often than not our spiritual enemy, the prince of darkness, is instigating what's weighing them down. Far too often the wives of such men are under similar attack.

"For we are not contending against flesh and blood," writes Paul, "but against the principalities, against the powers, against the world rulers of this present darkness, against the spiritual hosts of wickedness in the heavenly places" (Eph. 6:12).

That's why this same man also wrote, "Brethren, pray for us, that the word of the Lord may speed on and triumph" (2 Thess. 3:1).

He sent a letter to the Romans and said, "I appeal to you, brethren, by our Lord Jesus Christ and by the love of the Spirit, to strive together with me in your prayers to God on my behalf" (Rom. 15:30).

He wrote from prison to the Philippians, "I know that through your prayers and the help of the Spirit of Jesus Christ this will turn out for my deliverance" (1:19).

Here's another verse: "Continue steadfastly in prayer, being watchful in it with thanksgiving; and pray for us also, that God may open to us a door for the word, to declare the mystery of Christ, on account of which I am in prison" (Col. 4:2-3).

I testify to this same need, not only personally but for all my brothers and sisters in ministry. I've experienced my calling long enough to know that I'm not persuasive or clever or articulate or imaginative enough to convict beyond the surface, to draw people to Christ apart from the Spirit, to set in motion a divine moving of God. I desperately need the prayers of the Lord's people.

Like Paul, I say, "Brethren, pray for us, that the Word of the Lord may speed on and triumph" (2 Thess. 3:1). I'm confident I also speak for the majority of my peers in the ministry.

"But I don't know what to pray about," you say.

All professions have occupational hazards. Here are some reoccurring problems for clergy and their spouses: overwork, handling too much criticism, handling too much praise, neglect of family, depression, limited finances, the slowness of the decision-making process in churches, loneliness. Most of you have had enough contact with ministers to add other things to the list. Have you ever prayed for your pastor in any of these areas, or for his wife, or for his children?

A good way to find out the specific prayer needs of a person is to ask. He or she may want time to respond intelligently or just to recover from the shock of your inquiry! But if he thinks you're even half serious, he'll get back to you with a list, believe me.

How long has it been since you prayed for your minister? A week, two weeks, a month, or more? How long since you interceded fervently on his behalf? Is there any connection between how most people answer this question and where we are in relationship to a spiritual awakening? More and more I feel *ministers must be upheld in prayer if God's Word is to triumph over evil.* Revival won't just happen in this land without thousands of preachers proclaiming God's truth in power in a new way. And that won't occur without countless people, such as yourself, turning from being passive critics and becoming active prayer supporters on behalf of God's chosen servants.

2

LEARNING ABOUT INTERCESSORY PRAYER

Is corporate success likely in an organization where the top executives have a poor self-image, are insecure, and feel like quitting more often than going on?

"Not really," you respond.

This negative description is not too unlike many pastors nowadays. How do I know? In recent years I've been invited to numerous ministers' conferences and spoken to literally thousands of clergymen. Granted, there are many exceptions, but the larger percentage are hurting badly in one way or another, and that often includes men in some of our stronger churches.

What's true regarding ministers is usually intensified in the lives of their wives. What a difficult role these spouses are called to fill! Behavior expectations are different in almost every parishioner's mind. Where is the school that adequately trains women for the unique problems they'll face both in the congregation and at home? How can she share the difficult lessons God is teaching her without risking the complaints of church members, such as, "She's out of place"?

Apart from the human factors, the greatest dilemma faced by the pastor's family is coping with the unseen foe. As soon as spiritual life begins to show itself in a church body, the enemy will automatically counter-attack. His favorite pattern has always been to annoy or harass leaders.

Perhaps lay people are less aware of this dynamic than those in our profession realize. Unfortunately, the feeling prevails that because ministers are "holy" people they don't have needs like common folk. Of course, we all understand there is no such thing as a bionic pastor, but this is the idea most church members have. At least, if the frequency of parishioners' prayers for their ministers are any indication, they must perceive his needs to be very few indeed.

"Do you sense your people adequately support you in prayer?" I often ask my ministerial peers.

"Not really," is usually what I hear.

"Maybe they do pray, and you just don't know it," I prod.

"No, I don't think so," they respond.

Do people in the average church pray for their minister? Do they really intercede? Do they plead on his behalf? I am convinced the answer is no, not because lay people are unspiritual or immature or carnal. The biggest block seems to be a lack of awareness regarding the urgency of such a need.

How can the church move forward aggressively if its

leaders aren't protected by the prayers of God's people? Apart from new life being breathed into God's ministers, the idea of a spiritual awakening is pretty much a pipe dream. That's more than a nice devotional thought. It's a vital truth that demands a response from each of us. The revival for which many of us long will not come without ministers who stand strong because they know that the intercession of their people has inhibited the ability of the enemy to thwart or damage or destroy what God has called them to do.

"Brethren, pray for us," writes Paul, "that the word of the Lord may speed on and triumph" (2 Thess. 3:1). Similar appeals can be found in well over half of his letters. Ministers must be upheld in prayer if God's Word is to triumph over evil.

Everyone agrees, but one major problem emerges as soon as you try to pray. "Father in heaven," you say, "I'm here on behalf of my minister to plead his cause before you. What I want to say about him is—ah, let's see. Just a minute now, I'm sure I'll think of something." Eventually you mumble, an embarrassed, "Please bless him real good, God. Amen." And you think that was sure a fiasco! At least I did it alone and not in a group.

It's a meaningless exercise to sustain a prayer burden for someone whose needs you can't even name. If we could just persuade ministers to share their requests, it would be beautiful. I'm not referring only to church needs. I'm talking about personal ones: "My wife and I are struggling financially. Both of us are tired and more crotchety than usual. For a while now the Bible seems to have lost its freshness."

"But won't that encourage gossip?" you ask.

No, just the opposite is true. Parishioners will have already been talking about the grouchiness and the way the family never buys any new clothes and the recent staleness of the preaching. Amazingly, admitting the need and making it a prayer request stops any gossip almost immediately.

But, let's assume your pastor isn't open to sharing his deepest burdens. I find the easiest way of unearthing another's true needs is through a series of empathetic questions. What are his responsibilities? What are his pressures? What are his weaknesses? What are his spiritual gifts? What are his dreams?

Let's say you want to pray intelligently for me, but don't know what to say to the Lord. Well, ask yourself some of these questions: What are David's responsibilities? You know enough to say at least, "Father, help him as he prepares broadcasts fifty-two weeks a year." Then elaborate some, "May he know what topics to choose. Give him insight in his preparation. Don't allow the broadcast to become routine to him. Keep every visit special."

What pressures does David face? Picture yourself trying to play back-up centerfield to Joe DiMaggio. Or to bring it a little closer home, how about being a new understudy in a congregation where a man has had an extremely successful thirty-nine-year pastorate?

Much of intercessory prayer is just getting into the other person's shoes for a while. If you could do that on my behalf, you would know I can't be John D. Jess, the founder and for almost forty years the director of the broadcast ministry I have inherited. Yet a pressure to match his skills is there, and it takes time to gain new friends to replace those who resent change. How I wish I could persuade some people to channel the energy of their understandable disappointment into supportive prayer, which I long for because I believe God called me to this position.

What are David's weaknesses? Do you feel I'm inexperienced at radio? Pray that God will speed up the learning process. If you received our newsletter and saw a picture of me and felt I was slightly overweight, then don't just write and vent. Pray that I will have more self-control. If you think I'm too gentle, ask God to give me boldness. Too hard to hear? Ask for better projection and enunciation. Sometimes too humorous? Pray for more sobriety. If you love me, please don't let my perceived weaknesses be discussed without praying over them also.

What are David's gifts? As a beginning, preaching and teaching. "And, Father, may he not speak just human thoughts but rather as Peter writes, 'the oracles of God.' Protect his gifts from the enemy. Keep him free from interruptions when preparing messages." Those who regularly preach or teach could be great intercessors in this area because they know what it is like.

What dreams does David have? You don't have to listen to me very often before you know my heart longs for a great spiritual awakening in this land. To bring that request before the Lord is to intercede on my behalf as well.

Have you got the idea? Apply this same technique to your prayer for your minister. Ask yourself questions: If the enemy attacks, in what area will he probably strike? What times of the week is the pastor most vulnerable?

In what areas does he feel most insecure? If he could change something about the church, what would it be? Has the family had any major disappointments? What's the hardest thing about his job?

If you don't know the answers, ask your minister. He'll probably find it easier to respond to your questions than to compile a list of prayer requests.

Now gather a group of spiritually concerned friends and hold a discussion on *"How We Can Better Pray for Our Pastor and His Wife."* Meet at home, not in a restaurant, so that you can spend a good portion of the time before the Lord. What a great evening that could be! And what a metamorphosis there would be in our churches!

I see men and women in ministry released from spiritual weariness. I hear sermons being preached with new power. I imagine countless conversations about "what's going on over at First Church." I envision the joy of the Lord permeating congregations all across this land. I picture numberless sanctuaries filled to overflowing. I can even fancy church business meetings being held in love, order, and brevity! I project many conversions and greater satisfaction because of rapid spiritual growth due to worship coming alive, and delight in service.

Take away concentrated intercession on behalf of the leaders and the picture fades. That's why *ministers must be upheld in prayer if God's Word is to triumph over evil.* It's hard work, but well worth it.

3

PRAYING FOR LEADERS

A story D. L. Moody liked to tell is found in the little book, *The Mighty Ministry of Intercession,* by James McClure. After the great Chicago fire Moody went to England for rest and to learn from the Bible scholars there. One Sunday morning he was persuaded to speak in a church in London. Unfortunately, everything about the service dragged, and Moody wished he had never consented to preach.

In the city there was an invalid woman who had heard of Moody's work in America. She had been asking God to send him to London. Her sister was present at the church that Sunday morning and upon returning home asked, "Guess who preached to us today?" One pulpit supply after another was named but none was correct. "Ah, ha," the questioner said. "It was Mr. Moody from Chicago."

Instantly the sick woman turned pale. "This is an answer to my prayer," she gasped. "But if I had known he was to be at our church I should have eaten nothing this morning but waited on God. Leave me alone. Don't let anyone come to see me. Do not send me anything to eat." And all that afternoon this saint gave herself to intercessory prayer.

As Moody preached that night he became conscious there was a different atmosphere in the church, for the power of God seemed to fall upon him and his hearers. As he drew to a close, he felt strongly led to give an invitation, asking all who would like to accept Christ to rise. Four or five hundred stood to their feet. Taken aback, Moody thought they must have misunderstood, so he put the question several ways. But, no, they had fully understood. He then requested that these people go to an adjoining room, and quietly queried the pastor as to who they all were.

"I don't know," said the minister.

"Are they your people?" probed Moody.

"Some of them."

"Are they Christians?"

"I don't think so."

In that adjoining room, Moody again strongly posed the question of faith in Christ. There were still just as many who rose. Confused, he instructed the inquirers to meet with their pastor the following night. The next day he left for Dublin, but as soon as he reached his destination he received a telegram from the pastor stating he must return immediately, for a great revival had commenced. There were more out the second night than the first!

This was the beginning of Mr. Moody's work as an international evangelist. Out of these early efforts came the religious awakening of Great Britain and Ireland and the salvation of thousands upon thousands of people throughout the world. How good it was for England and all Europe that this man preached! And how fortunate that one invalid had not ceased to pray for the ministry of God's servant as he opened the Word.

Stories not too dissimilar surround the ministry of Charles Finney, the man under whose preaching this country experienced some of her mightiest movings of God. Included in those spiritual success tales was one about a Mr. Abel Clary, who never appeared in public. Though educated and licensed to preach, his ministry was a silent one. Lying in bed with tuberculosis, he would draw a little table to his side and write in his journal day by day: "My heart has been moved to pray for Utica, for Syracuse, for Binghamton, for Rochester." After Mr. Clary's death, Finney, who had known him from boyhood, obtained his memorandum book and found that the sequence of blessing poured out upon his ministry was in the precise order of the burden laid upon that man's heart.

I suspect in heaven we'll discover that no great victories were ever won on this planet apart from someone paying the price in prayer.

Without a doubt this is one of the great lacks in our present society. There is so much to read, watch, listen to, and do that God's people don't know much about intercessory prayer anymore. This discipline has been lost to ABC Sports and situation comedies and magazines and the newspaper and the stereo and the hundreds of other infringements that in themselves certainly can not be called bad. But just between us, doesn't it seem like a long time since this land witnessed a great spiritual awakening? In terms of eternity, don't all these diversions seem superficial?

In the last two chapters I challenged you to begin interceding for the ministers in your life, to plead with God on their behalf. I reminded you that *ministers must be upheld in prayer if God's Word is to triumph over evil.* Now I suppose the big question is, "How have you been doing?" Have you made an attempt to be supportive?

In order to encourage you further, I have compiled some thoughts under the heading "Twenty-one Practical Suggestions on How to Uphold Your Ministers and Their Families in Prayer." Here they are:

Learning about Intercessory Prayer

1. Define the word *intercession* and write down three synonyms.

Intercession _____

_____

1. _____ 2. _____ 3. _____

2. Read a good book on intercessory prayer. I have always thought highly of E. M. Bounds's writings such as *The Weapon Of Prayer, Prayer and Praying Men, The Necessity of Prayer,* and *Power Through Prayer.* These are all available now in paperback (Baker, $1.45).

3. Ask someone skilled at praying for others to share with you lessons he or she has learned.

4. Attend a midweek service to see what you can pick up by observing how believers in the church pray

for your pastor and others.

5. Make a study of prayer requests for others by Bible greats such as Abraham, Moses, Samuel, Daniel, or Paul.

6. How do passages about the present intercessory ministry of Christ challenge you? (See Isa. 53:12, Rom. 8:34, and Heb. 7:25). Read John 17 for an example of Christ interceding for those he loves.

Discovering the Needs of Your Pastor and His Family

7. Call your minister or his wife and ask how you can be supportive of them in prayer (See #11 for questions).

8. If you aren't that bold, write a letter with the same intent and enclose a self-addressed, stamped envelope for a reply.

9. Contact someone less threatening who can tell you much of what you want to know concerning your pastor's needs.

10. Spend some time with church friends constructively discussing together what you think are valid prayer requests on behalf of your minister's family.

11. Set aside twenty minutes of quiet to figure out the prayer needs of your pastor and his household. Often it is helpful to approach the topic of prayer requests indirectly. Good questions for your minister might be the following:

- What do you find hardest about your job?
- If you could change one thing in the church, what would it be?
- How are your children doing?
- What are your good and bad days in the week?
- Can you share your vision for the church? Answers

to such inquiries should reveal specific prayer requests.

Setting Realistic Intercessory Prayer Goals

12. How much time do you feel you should invest each week in intercessory prayer for your preacher in order to be truly supportive? _____

13. Project how many weeks this ministry should continue before its effectiveness begins to make itself known. _____

Actually Doing the Job of Pleading for Your Minister's Cause

14. Keep an active list of what you desire to pray about between Mondays and Fridays in relationship to your minister. Choose the time(s) and place you want to talk to the Lord. If possible, when the hour arrives, have a pencil and paper handy to record problems, joys, answers, and lessons learned.

15. What special prayer plans do you have for Saturdays? How does this day differ for you from your pastor's, your pastor's wife, and your pastor's children?

16. When is the best time on Sunday for you to talk to God about the Lord's day duties of your pastor? What role will his wife play today at the home and in the church? Can you be a part of the early Sunday risers who through the years have held up the hands of God's servants? _____

17. What extra in-between times can you take advantage of throughout the week to remind God of your minister's needs? (Some times are while cleaning up, at prayers before meals, when driving, or during church services).

18. Have you considered fasting when a need is intense?

19. Is there value in forming a small band of church intercessors who separately or together commit themselves to pray regularly for your minister and his family? In time, could not the names of other ministers or church leaders be added to this list?

Reminders to Keep at It

20. Prayer reminders on three-by-five cards placed in strategic positions (mirror, refrigerator, desk, dashboard, briefcase) could prove helpful.

21. Putting your new prayer burden in writing and sending it to your pastor's home will not only seal your commitment, but greatly encourage this servant of the Lord as well.

4

REVIVE US AGAIN

"Lord, thou wast favorable to thy land," begins Psalm 85. The psalmist is looking back at the manner in which God had graciously brought healing to Israel in times past. "Wilt thou not revive us again, that thy people may rejoice in thee?" (v. 6).

This request was probably not too different from what was being prayed by believers across America as the 1700s were coming to a close. Far from the force it had been during the Great Awakening fifty years earlier, the influence of religion was now on the wane. Everyone's primary energies had been channeled into a war for independence, and the fact that numbers of ministers had sided with England obviously hadn't helped matters. This long military struggle also brought normal side effects, such as divisions within families and a general lowering of moral standards.

Because the French had greatly aided our war effort, the American susceptibility to the current anti-God philosophies of their allies also contributed to the waning influence of religion. European infidelity and skepticism soon came to reign in our colleges and to permeate American society as well. The attacking pen of freethinker Thomas Paine was extremely popular. All in all, true believers found themselves in a literal life-and-death struggle. No less a figure than Chief Justice John Marshall, a devout layman, wrote that in his opinion the church was far too gone to ever be revived.

The national scene was also one of confusion following the surprise victory at Yorktown in 1781. Unfortunately, a successful revolution had not issued in a newborn utopia. Rather, there was to be long labor before any semblance of order came in this birthing. The Articles of Confederation had proved unworkable over the eight long years before the adoption of our present constitution. Strong personalities vied for position. Arguments raged regarding boundaries as the population continued to grow. Secular historians reported 300,000 of the approximately 5 million were confirmed drunkards.

Frontiers like Kentucky and Tennessee were hotbeds of lawlessness and iniquity. And little wonder, when some areas with as many as 50,000 inhabitants had no preacher of any denomination. A committee of Congress reported on the shocking state of affairs in these western territories where only one court had been held in five years.

Desperate but not hopeless, in the winter of 1794 a group of twenty-three New England ministers issued a circular letter calling for a concert of prayer for spiritual awakening. Addressed to ministers and churches of all Christian denominations throughout the States, it suggested devoting the first Tuesday in January, 1795, and once a quarter thereafter to public prayer until the Almighty deigned to answer their pleas.

Apparently hearts were hungry because the response was enthusiastic. In the western territories covenants were entered into by Christian people to spend a whole day each month in prayer, plus a half hour every Saturday night and every Sunday morning. Seminary students met to study the history of revivals. Church members formed Aaron and Hur Societies to "hold up the hands of their ministers through intercession."

Stirrings began in the east, with God working in congregations in Connecticut, Massachusetts, New York, New Hampshire. "It is not necessary," writes the revival historian, Dr. J. Edwin Orr, of Fuller Seminary, "to detail reports of the awakenings in every Eastern state to confirm the claim that the Second Great Awakening was effective from Maine to Maryland."

Without emotional excesses, the blessing usually came in the context of normal church life, and unlike the outpourings of fifty years earlier, the leaders used by God were almost as numerous as the congregations experiencing the refreshing. Most startling were the accounts of established colleges in the east being restored to orthodox thinking.

In the west the manifestations were more spectacular. In July of 1798 communion was celebrated at tiny Red River, Kentucky, and James McGready, a Presbyterian, preached. Rough, like the people to whom he ministered, it's said he was so ugly he attracted attention on the street. On this occasion, his sermon brought much conviction. Was this, then, to be the answer to prayers that had now ascended throughout these regions for some three years?

A month later, at Gasper River, hearers actually fell prostrate on the ground, groaning in their conviction. Reported McGready, "The winter of 1799 was for the most part a time of weeping and mourning with the children of God. But during the summer of 1800 all previous revivals in the area seemed nothing more than a few scattered drops before a mighty rain." The Great Awakening in the west had begun, changing the frontier and the nation.

Oh, how I wish I could paint for you the scene of the camp meetings. Rev. Barton Stone, another Presbyterian minister of that period wrote:

A memorable meeting was held at Cane Ridge in August, 1801. The roads were crowded with wagons, carriages, horses and footmen moving to the solemn camp. It was judged that between 20,000 and 30,000 persons were assembled. Four or five preachers spoke at the same time in different parts of the encampment without confusion. The Methodist and Baptist preachers aided in the work and all appeared cordially united. We all engaged in singing the same songs, all united in prayer, all preached the same Gospel. The numbers converted will be known only in eternity. This meeting continued six or seven days and nights, and would have gone longer, but food for such a multitude failed. Many had come from Ohio and other distant points. They returned home and diffused the same spirit in their respective neighborhoods. So low had religion sunk and such carelessness had universally prevailed, I had thought that nothing common could have arrested and held the attention of the people.

Having studied the events in these settings, I'm not unaware of the charges of emotionalism. There is sufficient data to challenge that accusation, but space prevents a lengthy defense. Suffice it to say the renewal in the east took different forms when transferred to the frontier, but the results were the same.

Dr. George Baker wrote another doctor in a letter:

On my way, I was informed by settlers on the road that the character of Kentucky was entirely changed, and that they were as remarkable for sobriety as they had formerly been for dissoluteness and immorality. And indeed I found Kentucky to appearances the most moral place I had ever seen. A profane expression was hardly ever heard. A religious awe seemed to pervade the country.

Knowing I've not even touched on what God did in the south, I must now change the direction of my remarks. Let me state my case as the psalmist does: *Stirred by reviewing the past, God's people pray, "Revive us again!"*

It's no surprise to me that periods of spiritual awakening historically included a moving of God among members of the clergy. That makes sense, because how else can a revival be sustained? There would have to be preachers capable of teaching and training and inspiring. Conversely, if there is a stirring of the Spirit among ministers, can it be long before the people begin to respond? The two go together.

"Daddy," said my son the other morning as we looked into an empty refrigerator and tried to figure out what we'd fix for breakfast, "if we had some ham, we could have ham and eggs—if we had some eggs!" And we laughed. But it was true. To accomplish some jobs certain ingredients are absolutely essential. And a revived church requires leaders who are on fire for the Lord.

Narrowed to this scope then, I can speak with some authority because I have frequent contact with fellow ministers. In many ways I believe the scene is far more positive than it was, say, ten years ago. Granted, some denominations have received a lot of publicity for opening their doors to the ordination of people who excuse what I personally believe the Scriptures call sin. Now and again, one hears stories of certain men of the cloth who fall prey to one kind of vice or another.

Yet overall, the picture is optimistic. Conservative seminaries are booming, countless books on the local church have helped correct problems of long standing, and increased communication between various denominations has had a balancing effect on our profession. Were it not for one noticeable lack, I think we might be close to a breakthrough among the clergy.

I feel strongly that ministers today lack the prayer support they most desperately need in order to serve effectively in the spiritual realm. Without that support, it's like a businessman trying to operate with no capital or a housewife cooking and cleaning with no access to water. Prayer is essential for spiritual ministry. Everyone agrees, but unfortunately very few people involve themselves in this ministry on behalf of their ministers beyond a superficial God-bless-our-pastor.

If only a third of the time church people spent criticizing their minister could be invested in serious prayer for him, it's highly conceivable many churches would come alive overnight.

And by no means am I trying to picture the clergy as being perfect. One of the biggest reasons such men need prayer is precisely because of their feet of clay.

The fact is, because of their position ministers are prime targets for the enemy. If you were Satan and wanted to neutralize the effectiveness of a given work that is starting to cause you problems, whom would you go after? How interesting that Christ said to Peter the evening of the Last Supper, "Simon, Simon, behold, Satan demanded to have you, that he might sift you like wheat" (Luke 22:31). Why wasn't Matthew or Andrew pegged for the attack? Because Peter was the leader, that's why. And how special that Christ adds, "But I have prayed for you that your faith may not fail" (v. 32).

So I'm suggesting we follow our Lord's example and pray for our spiritual leaders. My conviction is that ministers are a weather vane that indicates which direction spiritual winds are blowing. Therefore, when God's people seriously begin praying "Revive us again," it's not long before they become burdened for their pastors.

5

ZEAL FOR GOD'S HOUSE

One thing I've appreciated in my study of Christ over the years has been the many sides to his personality as revealed in the Bible. He cannot be programmed like a machine. Scriptural passages continually crop up which defy one's predetermined concept of our Lord. Look briefly at one such unusual passage (an occasion that is mentioned in all four Gospels) as Christ visits Jerusalem during the Passover season.

Frank G. Slaughter's book, *The Crown and the Cross*, describes what happened as follows:

This time Jesus did not go directly to the Porch of Solomon but entered the Temple market beneath the royal porch that formed the southern portico. Here the stalls for sellers of sacrificial animals occupied the entire southern wall of the Sanctuary area and, lining the inside aisle of this same section, were the booths of the moneychangers, each man sitting behind the heavy chest that held his stock of coins.

The yearly tax required by the Temple and all gifts had to be paid, according to religious law, in the Tyrian shekel. All other coins, whether the Roman denarius, the Persian doric, the mina, or any of the myriad coinage then in use, had to be changed into the approved shekel of Tyre. This was the province of the moneychangers who were allowed by law to make a small charge for their services. The law did not set the rate of exchange, however, so they did not scruple to bilk the pilgrims who flocked to Jerusalem from all parts of the world. The moneychangers shared a portion of their profits with the priests for the privilege of setting up their cabinets in the Temple.

Lines of waiting customers were standing at most of the booths when Jesus entered, and the heavy smell of smoke and burning flesh from the altars on the upper level hung over them like a pall. Jesus paused and his eyes swept the length of the market where a babble of voices rose as the constant haggling over prices and exchange rates went on. As he watched, his eyes began to smoulder with anger at the commercial prostitution of this edifice which had been dedicated to the glory of his Father. Striding forward purposefully, moving so quickly that even long-legged Peter increased his pace to keep up with him, Jesus reached the first booth. Stooping, he thrust his hands beneath the table, overturning it and scattering coins, coupons, and other articles upon the floor.

The disciples were aghast. They had never seen Jesus in this guise. But no one tried to hold him back as he strode on and seized another of the tables, upending it too and sending it crashing to the floor, nor did he respect the moneychangers. Stepping across to where one of them was haggling over the value of a coin with a pilgrim from Alexandria, he tumbled the heavy chest to the floor and sent the piles of coins spinning.

And now the disciples were infected by Jesus' forthright actions and themselves started overturning the booths around them. The sudden commotion brought the Temple guards, but they were unable to deal with so unusual a situation and hastily summoned one of the chief priests. That portly sybarite came in his rich vestments and the crowd opened a path for him to Jesus, where he stood, panting a little, his eyes still flashing with anger.

The rage in Jesus' eyes and the authority he radiated disconcerted even the haughty priest. Before he could speak Jesus lashed out at him, his ringing tones carrying to the farthest corner of the Temple area.

"It is written, 'My house is a house of prayer,' he accused the priest. "But you have made it a den of thieves."

The priest gave no answer and after a moment, the anger in Jesus' eyes died away. Abruptly he turned and, with the disciples hurrying after him, strode around the lower level of the east portico and Solomon's Porch where he had taught on other occasions. By now word had spread throughout the Temple that the prophet of Nazareth had overturned the tables of the moneylenders. No one doubted that the final test of strength between him and the authorities was near (World, 1959, pp. 335-337).

Here's a description of one of those rare times when Christ in his earthly pilgrimage through our toil and grief had just had it. Knowing what the temple meant in terms of his Father's relationship to mankind, plus the significance of the hour, it was almost as if something in him had snapped at sight of the abuse.

The account in John 2 differs slightly from the other three Gospels and therefore raises speculation as to whether this is the same incident or another, similar one. John writes about our Lord making a whip of cords and driving out all, including sheep and oxen. In this account his disciples remember the writings, "Zeal for thy house will consume me." Paraphrased, (Isa. 69:9; John 2:17) that expression might read: There is a passionate spirit within me concerning the sanctuary of the Lord.

Oftentimes of late I must confess wondering if we would see the same reaction if Christ were to visit personally many places of worship today. Would normal modern activities in his house trigger the same intense reaction? Let me be specific.

On the one day in seven divinely set aside for people to restore themselves spiritually, how do you think Christ would respond where a quarter or a third of the congregation arrived late for worship? This practice has become so accepted that bulletins indicate proper times during the service for such offenders to be seated.

What would Jesus say if it were made public that the greater number of those present had in no way prepared themselves to enter his Father's house? Up late the night before, most had grumpily rolled out of bed and dressed without any expectation whatsoever that the Creator of the world might maintain his normal habit and tabernacle with his people that day.

If reading had taken place earlier in the day, it was probably not the Scriptures but the Sunday newspaper. Cross words had perhaps been exchanged between family members. Congregational singing was entered into with little thought as to the meaning of the hymns. No more major decision was made during God's hour than where to go for lunch that would serve good food and not be too crowded or which sport spectacular to watch that afternoon on television.

Preaching is easily dismissed nowadays by playing the game of mentally agreeing how helpful or interesting the thoughts were. And-So-and-So was really (or really wasn't) good today. Are you ready to be caught up in the traditional ritual? Here's the call to worship: "The Lord is in his holy temple. *The Lord is in his holy temple.* Let all the earth keep silence. *Let all the earth keep silence before Him.* Keep silent. Keep silent before him." Aha! . . . Nice,—huh?

How do you feel about all this, Jesus?

Charles Finney, a thundering voice for God in the 1800s, lists evidences of a backslidden heart in his revival lectures. The first one is a manifest formality in religious exercises which he defines as "a stereotyped, formal way of saying and doing things, that is clearly the result of habit rather than the outgushing of the spiritual life."

In church services "the backslider in heart will pray or praise, confess, or give thanks with his lips, so that all can hear him, but perhaps in such a way that no one can feel him." This person finds religious duties a burden, but having promised to serve the Lord dares not back off from this commitment, and becomes "like a dutiful, but unloving wife," writes Finney, "who tries to do her duty to her husband, but fails utterly because she does not love him. Her painstaking effort to please her husband is constrained . . . and her relationship and duties become the burden of her life" (*Revival Lectures*. Revell, n.d., pp. 491-492).

Well, if you fit the description, Finney warns that you should face the fact that you're backslidden. And if these conditions prevail, the bigger part of the blame rests, not with the parishioners but with church leaders. Were Christ present in body would he approve of the sermons preached today? Would he be pleased with thoughts supposedly spoken on behalf of the eternal God that were not grounded in the truth of Scripture, bathed in prayer, composed with extreme care, or, because of the urgency of the hour, preached with a broken heart?

Would the lack of concern shown so often by careless service planning trouble him? Or would he be disturbed by the casual attitude on the part of many who walk on the platform to minister, oblivious to the fact that there are individuals in the congregation around whose lives eternity itself hangs in the balance? What about musicians who place more emphasis on performance, appearance, and personality than upon being righteous vessels the Lord himself can indwell?

Christ must be weary of church school teachers who can spend twenty to thirty hours a week watching television and still excuse poor lessons because they are "too busy." How does he feel toward people in church governing positions who allow their human personality to dominate meetings because they aren't walking close enough to the Lord to discern the promptings and the checkings of the Holy Spirit? What of folk who serve Communion or usher or do janitorial tasks but who always have to be handled with kid gloves when a change is desired because they don't like being inconvenienced?

If I sound too harsh it may be because I've disciplined myself for years to recognize the presence of Christ whenever I am in a position of ministry. As I sit in the broadcasting studio, I am not alone. Jesus hears every word. While there is no greater joy than sensing I have represented him well, I have also experienced no greater pain than feeling I have spoken poorly on his behalf.

May I suggest that you take this Guest with you to church on Sunday. I realize the act will have to be done in your imagination, or maybe I should say by faith, which is the conviction of things not seen, according to Hebrews 11.

Create a special place where you can mentally invite Christ to join your company on the way to church. From that moment on, be as conscious of what happens as you would were a neighbor accompanying you. Observe what transpires from Christ's imagined reaction. Once seated, reserve enough space for Jesus to sit next to you. Begin writing notes and evaluate from his mindset what is good or bad in the morning's event. Be critical of your participation in the service. If the morning is perfect, the exercise will only enhance your appreciation of your home congregation. If much is left to be desired, you have at least begun to get a handle on what can be done about it.

To follow closely after Christ is to be marked by a zeal for God's house! Like your Master, are you characterized by a passionate spirit regarding the sanctuary of the Lord?

6

CHRISTIAN CRITICS

"I believe you beautiful people are a church with which God himself is pleased." How would you like to be part of a congregation receiving a commendation like that? Especially if the words came from the lips of the great missionary, Paul.

Though that precise compliment doesn't appear in the Bible, by reading between the lines you get the impression that such were the apostle's sentiments regarding the church at Philippi. Founded during his second extensive missionary journey, it included members such as Lydia, the seller of purple goods; a demon-possessed slave girl who was being used by opportunists to make money telling fortunes; and a jailer converted following the famous midnight earthquake. Most Bible commentators agree that of all the churches Paul planted, this was the one in which he took the most pride.

Now these special friends had once again been gracious to him. Knowing he was imprisoned in Rome, they had sent Epaphroditus over many hundreds of miles with a love gift to help meet the personal needs of this man who had first shared with them about the Christ. When it was time for their representative to return home, Paul used the occasion to write to the Philippians the letter we find in the New Testament under that name. Even now, the love relationship is apparent in the correspondence. In many ways these people were his ideal church. But apparently Paul had picked up something in his conversations with Epaphroditus, so he also adds a warning. Several times he mentions the need for oneness and unity.

Fully aware that the enemy works overtime at setting believers against each other and perceiving the negative role a critical spirit plays in that routine, Paul is anxious that such a spirit not have a climate in which to grow at Philippi. Tucked into his message at several points are words like these: "Only let your manner of life be worthy of the gospel of Christ, so that whether I come and see you or am absent, I may hear of you that you stand firm in one spirit, with one mind striving side by side for the faith of the gospel" (1:27). "Do nothing from selfishness or conceit, but in humility count others better than yourselves" (2:3). In other words, don't let your ego get wrapped up in what you are doing. "I entreat Euodia and I entreat Syntyche to agree in the Lord" (4:12).

And finally, the long sentence around which I have chosen to center my immediate remarks: "Do all things without grumbling or questioning, that you may be blameless and innocent, children of God without blemish in the midst of a crooked and perverse generation, among whom you shine as lights in the world, holding fast the word of life, so that in the day of Christ I may be proud that I did not run in vain or labor in vain" (2:14-16).

Paul desired that this congregation, a model in so many ways, would remain exemplary. In order for that to happen, they must be very careful not to allow the sin of criticism to invade their ranks. His warning and my thoughts can be summarized as follows: *Fulfilling God's ideal includes guarding against a critical spirit.*

Now criticism per se is not always evil. Some of the greatest periods of church history were the result of complaints against abuses. Jesus himself found much fault with the religious leaders of his day and was quite vocal about it. But carping is never regarded, even for a moment, as a characteristic of our Master. Though they were dubbed protestors or protestants, history books record the positive contributions the reformers made. Their complaints were not an end in themselves, but merely a backdrop against which to set the context in which events transpired. No one has the feeling that these people sought the critic's chair. Rather, complaints were more generally mixed with loving tears.

So I am convinced that Paul was referring in these verses to a basic spirit of criticism, grumbling, complaining, or murmuring (depending on your version of Scripture) and arguing, or wrangling, disputing, questioning. These words immediately conjure up the picture of Old Testament Israel during Moses' time. Despite the phenomenal manner in which he carried out the Exodus assignment under God, there were always grumblings of discontent.

"Why have you brought the assembly of the Lord into this wilderness, that we should die here, both we and our cattle? And why have you made us come up out of Egypt, to bring us to this evil place? It is no land for grain, or figs, or vines, or pomegranates; and there is no water to drink" (Num. 20:5). Sound familiar?

The murmuring didn't stop when Moses died. It continued under the judges, the kings, the prophets, and the Messiah, and unfortunately it appeared often in what Paul refers to in Galatians as the Israel of God, the New Testament church. Even in this day, I have watched beautiful works toppled by this infernal plague and observed contemporary Moses-like leaders groaning under the weight of its relentless impact. Certainly you wouldn't be one of that stripe, would you? If the finger of God were to point out all those who had crossed the line of helpful and loving comments and wandered into the territory of hairsplitters and grumblers and the core of the critical, it wouldn't point you out, would it?

Fellow Christian, you have been hurt, I know; but I trust that you are not nursing the poison of past pains. I have seen enough of what cherishing grievances can do to sour the soul. If you could hear them, would others say that a critical spirit now characterizes you?

"I don't know," you respond, "but I am feeling guilty all of a sudden, and I do admit that the way this certain person in our church acts upsets me a great deal. Are you saying, David, that I have to affirm what he is doing in his role of leadership?"

No. Before you start verbally undermining him, however, let me offer some safeguards, and it is important that you hear these because what we are dealing with is a little like a neutron bomb. Once detonated, it tends to leave the building standing, but the living are decimated.

So first of all, check out your relationship with God. Are you spending time in Scripture and prayer? I personally fear well-intentioned people who aren't meeting regularly with the Lord. The self is deceptive and should not be trusted in stress situations. If there isn't a closeness in your walk with Christ, exercise extreme caution in speaking negatively about a fellow member of the body, especially a leader. Until you are again comfortable in your spiritual walk, listening is a safer policy lest you unwittingly grieve the Holy Spirit.

The second suggestion is to determine whether your consternation is over a matter of style or sin. It is hardly worth risking the holocaust that unchecked criticism can bring to the church if your differences are in the category of style.

Leadership personalities, whether they be pastors, elders, or committee chairpersons, vary from the extremely forceful to those who do little more than moderate where the group wants to go. None of these patterns is inherently wicked.

In my years of experience in the local church, which includes pastoring and consulting work, I have come to believe that most congregational squabbles are over matters of opinion. Probably any one of a number of views would work if everyone involved would agree to it.

In fact, most (not all, but most) issues that divide

church governing groups could be resolved by one of a dozen different ways. When people fight for their position they begin to line up as opponents rather than fellow team members. The vote is finally taken and the victor declared, but instead of unanimity in victory there is disunity and fragmentation. A group has become more fascinated with winning a vote than in doing the work its action requires. Worse yet, the victors must now activate the proposal under the constant harassment of a minority who have assumed the roles of enemy guerrilla fighters. And all the time the decision probably wasn't of vital significance to begin with.

If an issue clearly involves sin, it should not be excused. But a good rule of thumb to follow when there is a difference over matters of style is: If a group can't agree with enthusiasm, submit to the wishes of the recognized leader. Say, "Though it is not what I prefer, because someone must give leadership to us as a group, I am willing to back that plan which you feel is right."

A third checkpoint before starting down the path of unbridled criticism (I use that term because once you start grumbling about somebody, it is very hard to stop, right?) is to ask yourself, *have I honestly tried to resolve this issue by talking to the other party involved?*

When I have asked a person with a gripe, "Have you talked it out with them so that you clearly understand why they feel the way they do?" I am amazed by how few times people respond in the affirmative. A direct approach is apparently unthinkable. The pattern is to continue to discuss one's discontent with everyone *except* the proper party, and in effect a massive web of misunderstanding, and hard feelings is spun.

Now, I can't guarantee that time spent together will settle your differences, but at least it ought to settle in your mind whether the problem is a matter of style or of sin, and under whose leadership you see the issue to be falling.

A final caution: Before talking with others about this difficult, oh, let's face it—hard-headed, manipulating, do-it-my-own-way-or-else-pain-in-the-neck, ask, *Am I willing to bring the name of this person before my heavenly Father several times, sincerely asking God's very best for him or her?* Too many who know the Scriptures on this point don't practice them.

"But you ought to hear what they're saying about me!" you protest. Remember the old spiritual?

You can talk about me just all you please.
I'll talk about you down on my knees.

What I'm trying to do is delay on your part any bent toward the spirit of criticism because I know the toll those who travel its route must pay. Surely this is what Paul had in mind when he wrote that letter to the Philippian Christians, about whom he felt so warmly. Nip in the bud those problems that carry the potential for great harm among you, and know that fulfilling God's ideal includes guarding against a critical spirit.

7

HANDLE WITH RESPECT

I often wonder if I would be able to recognize a prophet were I to see one. The thought has come to me several times as I read sections of Scripture like the account of Stephen's defense just prior to his stoning. "You always resist the Holy Spirit," he insists. "As your fathers did, so do you. Which of the prophets did not your fathers persecute?" (Acts 7:51, 52). You know what Jesus said to the scribes and Pharisees, "Hypocrites! for you build the tombs of the prophets and adorn the monuments of the righteous, saying, 'If we had lived in the days of our fathers, we would not have taken part with them in shedding the blood of the prophets.' Thus you witness against yourselves" (Matt. 23:29-31).

Historically, it seems that prophets have not been the most popular of figures. But would I be included among those who turn a deaf ear to such a voice today? Would I recognize a prophetic message if I heard one? Can a prophet be spotted by his appearance? And how does an individual keep from being duped by a false seer? Do you ever wonder about such things? Questions like this sent me on a recent search through the Scriptures.

To begin with, there is no prophetic stereotype in the Bible. Prophets vary a great deal in personality, dress, position, and scope of ministry. For example, Daniel, a diplomatic statesman, is not at all like Elijah, who is almost a recluse. Jonah differs greatly from John the Baptist. Some prophets exercised an exclusively prophetic role, while others were also priests, such as Ezekiel, public officials, as was David, and judges such as Deborah, a prophetess. A conclusion I have drawn is that the average prophet did not stand out as weird or mysterious. More than likely he appeared as normal as the average person. Therefore, I've put away the notion that if one of God's prophets were to appear in our society he would resemble Merlin the magician.

Nor were the biblical prophets superhuman. Yes, some performed miracles. But they also sinned, like Abraham. You remember God's words to Abimelech, "Restore the man's wife; for he is a prophet" (Gen. 20:7). Moses lost his temper and Scripture records, "There has not arisen a prophet since in Israel like Moses" (Deut. 34:10). Samuel was impressed by outward appearances. Nathan was corrected by God regarding his endorsement of David to build the temple. Elijah was discouraged. John the Baptist wavered in his belief about Christ. They were all flawed by their humanity except of course, the greatest of the prophets, our Lord, who was also the unique Son of Almighty God.

Hebrews 1:1 reads: "In many and various ways God spoke of old to our fathers by the prophets" (Heb. 1:1). "Many and various" sums up what is being said so far. The prophets of Scripture don't fit into one mold as stargazers, or dashing superheroes, or desert wizards. What then binds them together?

Maybe Deuteronomy 18 helps. It reads in part: "The Lord said . . . , 'I will put my words in his mouth, and he shall speak to them all that I command him' " (v. 18). That pretty well summarizes the prophetic calling. A prophet is someone given a message to deliver on behalf of the Lord. One didn't become a prophet by birth, as did the priests born into the tribe of Levi. He was not like the royal son, next in line to the crown when his father, the king, dies. God chose his prophets individually to share his Word faithfully with the people.

At this point maybe I should also attack a further misconception. When people hear the word *prophet* they almost automatically think of someone who predicts the future. Often that was a part of the word God wanted spoken; but primarily the prophet was known as one who publicly spoke forth God's truth. Whether or not it was predictive was a matter of secondary importance.

About four hundred years prior to the birth of Christ the prophets of Israel ceased. Till that time there had been an almost uninterrupted flow of such voices. Then with the emergence of John the Baptizer, a new era was introduced and, of course, Christ was its central figure. In the New Testament the prophetic role burgeons. In fact, percentage wise, it contains as many references to prophets and prophecy as the Old Testament does. Aside from the obvious prophetic stance of a John, or a Paul, or a Peter, others included Zachariah, Agabus, Barnabas, Lucius, Silas, and the daughters of Philip, the evangelist.

Also, the term is often mentioned in passages about the gifts of the Holy Spirit. For example, "And his gifts were that some should be apostles, some prophets, some evangelists, some pastors and teachers . . ." (Eph. 4:11). Another reads, "Having gifts that differ according to the grace given us, let us use them: if prophecy, in proportion to our faith" (Rom. 12:6).

I can't help but feel that there are significant differences between the prophets in the Old Testament and prophecy as a gift of the Spirit today. At the same time, there are also some similarities. Understanding the kind of messages the biblical prophets gave should help us to be more discerning when that gift is exercised under the Spirit today. Just because someone stands behind a pulpit or before a microphone does not automatically qualify that person for the role of which I speak. On the other hand, I would hope and pray the gift hasn't vanished completely from the present church.

The Apostle Paul writes, "Do not despise prophesyings" (1 Thess. 5:20). In the Amplified Bible this short four-word verse comes out this way: "Do not spurn the gifts and utterances of the prophets—do not depreciate prophetic revelations nor despise inspired instruction or exhortation or warning." I think I can sum up Paul's thought as follows: "Don't despise those possessing the gift of prophecy." Stated positively: *"Treat those pos-*

sessing the gift of prophecy with highest esteem."

Qualities which consistently characterize prophetic voices, and therefore may be used as a measuring device when I'm asking myself if this is a valid prophet who needs to be respected, are the following:

Biblical prophets are characterized by (1) a message of rebuke, reform, and warning. That's so apparent I hardly need illustrate. Sin, repentance, and judgment are oft-recurring words. Here, of course, is where the prophet gets himself into trouble. "Your hands are full of blood . . ." wrote Isaiah. "Remove the evil of your doings from before my eyes; . . . If you refuse and rebel, you shall be devoured by the sword; for the mouth of the Lord has spoken" (Isa. 1:15-20). The cartoonist's drawing of a man carrying a sign reading "Repent!" or "The world is coming to an end!" is not totally unfair.

Yet, to emphasize only this dimension is lopsided, because true biblical prophets are also consistently characterized by (2) giving a word of comfort, encouragement, and hope. Here is where, in my mind, so many supposedly current prophetic voices fall short of their predecessors. They lack compassion. Knowing how to thunder, they have not yet learned to weep. It's only with a sorrowful heart that a good parent resorts to extreme measures of discipline. I'm leery of those who seem to enjoy the role of "God's critic." Is it conceivable there's a little too much of Jonah in them yet? So I look for the touch of comfort, encouragement, and hope for the faithful tucked into the message of rebuke, reform, and warning.

(3) Biblical prophets are characterized by the elevating of God's name and God's character and God's will.

They do more than wonder how people are responding to them personally. They make known the greatness and the goodness, the holiness and wrath and mercy and love and patience of the Lord, whose ways are high above the petty doings of the people or nations to whom the prophet addresses himself on behalf of God. In this context, prophets interpret history—past, present, and future—as seen from God's perspective.

Biblical prophets are (4) characterized by a consistent promise of the Messiah who will come. Certainly this is true throughout the Old Testament. But as you reflect on the New Testament you're quickly aware that this theme continues in predictions of the Second Coming of the Lord. "The Lord is not slow about his promise . . ." writes Peter, "but is forbearing toward you, not wishing that any should perish . . . But the day of the Lord will come . . ." (2 Pet. 3:9-10).

Biblical prophets are (5) characterized by a great urgency and godly fear. Like Ezekiel, they are watchmen upon whose hands eternally is the blood of those not warned of the Lord's thoughts. Like Isaiah, they will even go around naked if God is the one who says they are to do so.

And finally, biblical prophets are (6) characterized by imagination and skill in delivery. Almost without exception, members of this group are literary and easy to listen to. They make extensive use of the dramatic and the symbolic and the artistic, which communicates well with their hearers.

My hope is that with the help of such characteristics, we can together in our day treat those possessing the gift of prophecy with highest esteem.

8

A WORD TO MINISTERS

Most people pursue certain vocations because of money, status, benefits, personal fulfillment, individual skills, security, or parents' wishes. With one profession, however, all these issues play a secondary role, with vocational choice determined above all else by a rather mysterious element termed *a call*.

The vocation to which I'm referring, of course, is the ministry, and a call to it is a strong awareness that God himself has singled one out to work on his behalf.

Though not necessarily as dramatic as, for instance, Saul's blinding by Christ's glory on the Damascus road, *nevertheless* the conviction that such a spiritual affirmation has taken place is very real. In fact, so seriously is it regarded that to walk away from a divine commissioning would be tantamount to Jonah refusing God's assignment to preach at Nineveh.

Believers other than preachers sometimes experience calls to other vocations—medicine, business, counseling, music, obviously missionary work. But few professions revere this uppermost priority as much as do those going into full-time ministry. After examining a candidate's training and experience and spiritual gifts, invariably someone on an ordination council will ask the prospective preacher, "How do you know that God himself has *called* you to be one of his spokesmen?"

I suppose we ministers view our calls more seriously than the rest of society sees them. We identify with Paul's words, "As men of sincerity, as commissioned by God, in the sight of God we speak in Christ" (2 Cor. 2:17). Yet what we think hardly reflects the mood of the average person.

Take a poll around the country regarding which professions are most important and the results would show that ministers do poorly compared to doctors, lawyers, politicians, scientists, teachers, entertainers, writers, and newsmen. I presume it would have been a different story a hundred or two hundred years ago.

This drop of ratings in the eyes of the world, plus an imagined or possibly real lack of respect even among parishioners, has placed many ministers in a position where there is a wide gap between what they believe in their heads regarding their importance and what they feel in their emotions.

Certainly if God were to rank professions according to their worth, he would place the called ministers right at the top. After all, what is the success of the kingdom without us? That's not just my opinion, either.

Paul said, "And God has appointed in the church first

apostles, second prophets [or inspired proclaimers of his truth], third teachers [again of the Word], then worker of miracles, then healers, helpers, administrators" (2 Cor. 12:28).

Despite God's opinion, negative human voices can still effectively overshadow one's confidence in the importance of one's calling. My fear is that this is exactly what is happening.

I spend a great deal of time with men in the ministry, individually, on retreats, and at conferences. My wife would affirm that I feel most at home among fellow ministers. I'm alarmed by the number of men I meet in my profession who are discouraged, disillusioned, worn-out, confused, and lacking the optimism with which they first began. Of course, there are exceptions. Thank God for every such man who senses he's deeply loved and supported and doing a significant work.

I highly suspect, however, that far too many ministers act apologetically because the society in which they operate conditions them to see who they are as relatively unimportant. Are clergymen world changers? Yes, in the scheme of Christianity, but not in terms of what happens on the evening news or the front pages of the newspapers.

It's as though the battles we've fought, the lives that have been salvaged, the marriages saved, the constant salting of society with goodness, the weekly inspiration of an incredible number of sermons, the comforting of the sick, encouraging of the weak—all these receive scant attention on the part of the world. Anyone in a position of working hard at a task most people view as insignificant is bound to feel inferior sooner or later.

Without a doubt this attitude in these times is ironic. When God's ministers are better equipped to serve than any previous generation, the very role they are now so well prepared to fill is increasingly in question.

My suspicion is that it's been this way throughout history more often than not, which is the reason pastors or evangelists sometimes need to be encouraged in what they are doing. Though details are not explained, I suspect this was the case with a minister by the name of Archippus. In a letter to Philemon Paul calls him "our fellow soldier" (v. 2). The reference I had in mind, however, is in Colossians. In the final sentence before Paul completes this correspondence, he pens these words, "And say to Archippus, 'See that you fulfil the ministry which you have received in the Lord'" (4:17). Archippus, you've been chosen by God for leadership in the kingdom. Now, whatever the reason for slacking off, back to work! Fulfill your ministry.

This is not the only such reference I could cite. The same flavor is found in the better known letters to Timothy. "Rekindle the gift of God that is within you through the laying on of my hands" (2 Tim. 1:6). Paul continued, "I charge you in the presence of God and of Christ Jesus who is to judge the living and the dead, and by his appearing and his kingdom: preach the word, be urgent in season and out of season, convince, rebuke and exhort, be unfailing in patience and in teaching. . . . Always be steady, endure suffering, do the work of an evangelist," and here is that phrase again, "fulfill your ministry" (2 Tim. 4:1-5).

What I'm saying can be summed up in a sentence: *A*

minister sometimes needs a reminder of the importance of fulfilling his God-assigned work.

My purpose for this chapter is to sound words that are not proclaimed often enough. Eternity will reveal that the wars, treaties, personalities, inventions, conferences, convocations, or armistices that dominate history books were not really the events around which the world revolved! Instead, the great war between the kingdoms of light and darkness was central to all that was happening. The key which determined the direction of all that unfolded was the spirit of those called by God to serve him as ministers. Did they maintain the attitude of Paul, who wrote:

Having this ministry by the mercy of God, we do not lose heart (2 Cor. 4:1). Not that we are competent of ourselves to claim anything as coming from us; our competence is from God, who has made us competent to be ministers of a new covenant (2 Cor. 3:5-6). For what we preach is not ourselves, but Jesus Christ as Lord, with ourselves as your servants for Jesus' sake (2 Cor. 4:5). But what we are is known to God. . . . Working together with him, then, we entreat you not to accept the grace of God in vain (2 Cor. 5:11, 6:1).

Well, such a mindset is indeed rare throughout the ranks nowadays, isn't it? How can it be changed? How can this sense of destiny again be restored to God's ministers? One way is through encouraging words from parishioners. Ultimately, however, conditions will alter when those servants called by God perceive the uniqueness of their role and play the man. That's why I find it important to begin the day with a prayer something like this:

> Father, I can't expect the world to affirm the importance of what I do today. Because my knee is bowed before your Son, Jesus, there's little agreement between me and society regarding values. Even some believers don't understand my call.
>
> But once again this morning I commit myself and all of my gifts exclusively to the cause of your kingdom. By faith, I devote myself anew to spiritual warfare, following the example of Christ himself.
>
> My sights are set on rewards other than what can be achieved in this life. So meet my needs as promised while I again seek to serve you. *Amen.*

Such an approach restores my perspective. I need this regularly because, as a minister, I'm *not* in step with most other people. If the role is sometimes difficult, I can't expect the world to change its viewpoint regarding my profession. The turnabout must come from within me.

I'm hoping, of course, that this will be the case with many. While experiencing the privilege of being called by God to unique service, and knowing the support of God's people, it would be a tragedy not to fulfill our appointed ministry.